IMAGES OF ENGLAND

WHITNASH

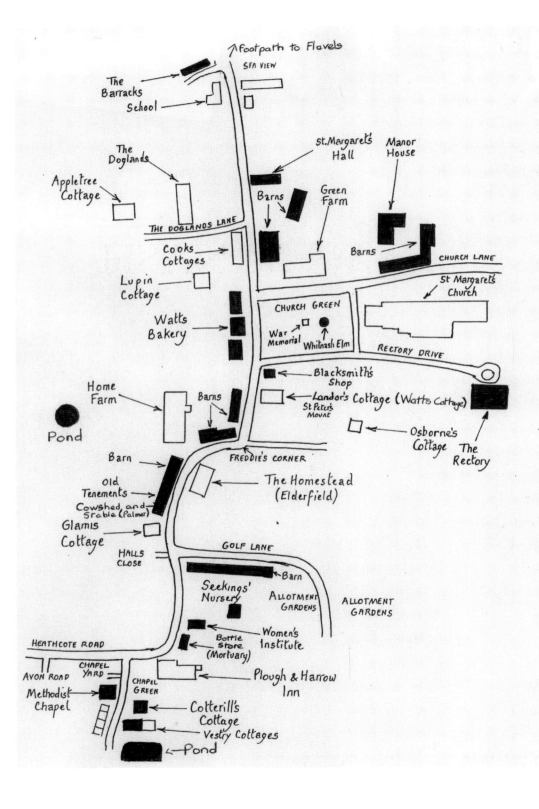

IMAGES OF ENGLAND

WHITNASH

JEAN FIELD

TEMPUS

St Margaret's Church there was an ancient pollard elm tree, such trees being said to signify the existence of a very long-established settlement. Tradition said that this tree was 1,000 years old.

Most of the half-timbered houses still left in Whitnash date from the seventeenth century, although parts of the Manor House, demolished in 1959, were probably older. St Margaret's Church was partially rebuilt in Victorian times, although the tower dates from around 1500.

One of the most colourful periods in Whitnash history was 1846-84, when the charismatic Canon James Reynolds Young was Rector. He helped organise the enclosure of the fields (Whitnash was one of the last places in England in this respect), ran a preparatory school for the sons of the nobility and printed some of the earliest parish magazines in the country.

Traditionally most of the inhabitants of Whitnash worked on the land, but in 1833, when the Flavel family opened a new iron-foundry to manufacture kitchen ranges, about a mile away, close to the canal in south Leamington, some Whitnash men found employment there. Today, over 200 years after the Flavel family first came to Leamington, the Eagle Foundry, now called Rangemaster, still provides employment for numerous Whitnash people. Few books have mentioned much about the history of Flavels, so a section of this publication will be devoted to this fascinating story.

The family of the writer Walter Savage Landor, who was born in Warwick in 1775, had many connections with Whitnash. A younger brother, Henry Eyres Landor, became Lord of the Manor of Whitnash in 1826 and the family connection continued long after his death in 1866. H.E. Landor owned numerous farms, which had previously belonged to his mother's family, and in 1860 he built and endowed a new village school, which is still in use as a church centre.

One glance through the photographs in this book will confirm the fact that in many ways the history of Whitnash is typical of other small towns in England. The area around St Margaret's Church is now a conservation area and the owners of the historic black and white houses which remain are rightly proud of the history of their properties. While many of the photographs in this book are of times long gone, a few illustrate the last decade in Whitnash history, which has been so important. It has been said, and the continued sale of new houses would seem to indicate this, that whilst many move to live in Whitnash, relatively few move out until forced by old age or circumstance to do so.

Jean Field
January 2005

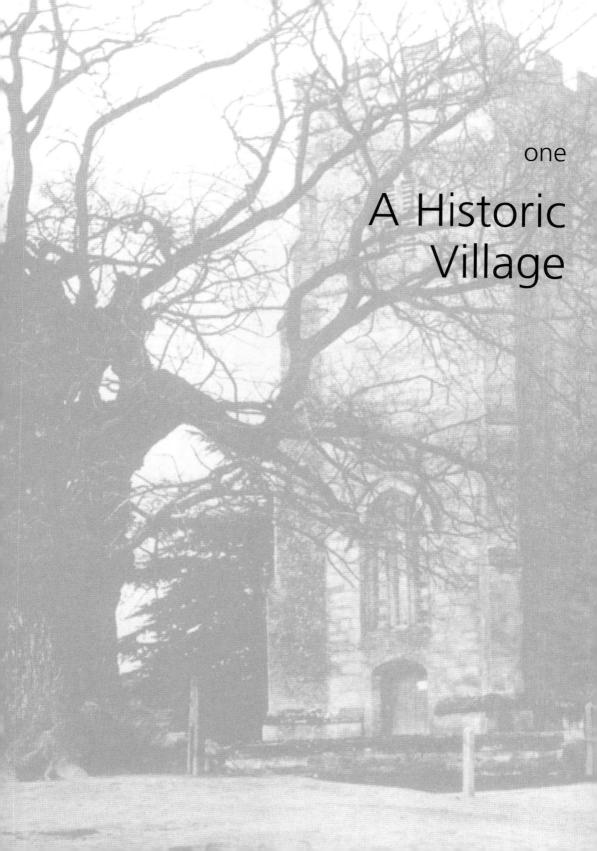

one

A Historic
Village

Whitnash Church and the village green as drawn by George Barnard in the early nineteenth century. The ancient pollard elm stands in front of the church, with the Glebe House visible behind. On the left are the Manor House and a couple of barns, with Green Farm on the extreme left. With a population of little over 200, Whitnash was then a secluded rural parish. There was a good water supply in the form of wells and springs, and in general the fields were extremely fertile. Most of the population worked on the land, yet extreme poverty was very rare. When Revd James Reynolds Young became Rector in 1846, the population had risen to over 300, and changes were imminent.

Opposite: A cover from a Whitnash Parish Magazine in 1867. Canon Young first helped to bring about the Act for the enclosure of the fields of Whitnash in 1850 and then he organised the rebuilding of the chancel of St Margaret's Church in 1855. In 1859 he began printing some of the earliest parish magazines in the country. The buildings portrayed on the woodcut are: Rose Cottage; the village school and the Barracks; the church and old elm tree; the Glebe House; and the Victorian Rectory.

The
Whitnash
Parish
Magazine.

No. ci.

May,
1867.

11

Looking north towards Leamington in 1821. Part of Green Farm is visible on the right, and a barn is behind the house. Cooks Cottages, before they were partially rebuilt in Victorian times, are on the left. At this time there was no road into Leamington from this part of Whitnash, apart from an ancient track, which went directly across fields to the point where the ladder bridge crossed the canal in Leamington adjacent to the site where the Flavel family later set up their foundry.

Mary Parker outside her cottage in around 1910. The cottage, situated at the bottom of Doglands Lane, housed two families, with the other entrance being below the canopy (complete with birdcage) in the centre. Water came from a pump and there was a shared outside toilet, a 'two-holer' for an adult and child. The buckets underneath were emptied weekly by the local council. Apple Tree Cottage, as the property became known, still survives.

Above: The Doglands,
c. 1906. These half-timbered
seventeenth-century dwellings
in Whitnash Road still
survive, looking much as
they did a century ago, but
the outbuildings have been
demolished. Doglands Lane is on
the extreme left.

Right: This oil painting by
E.M. Smith, dated 1877, depicts
the end section of The Doglands.
The building on the extreme
left was a washhouse.

Canon Young, Rector of Whitnash from 1846–84.
He was a great classical scholar and ran a small
preparatory school for the sons of the nobility in
the Rectory. The boys in his school helped him
to print the parish magazines and other items.

This is believed to be Ruth Young, the second
daughter of Canon Young, in the 1870s. She
raised money for the rebuilding of St Margaret's
Church by selling paintings she had completed,
and she was much involved in village life.

Robert Eyres Landor, *c.* 1861. Robert became Lord of the Manor of Whitnash in 1866 on the death of his brother, Henry Eyres Landor. He was a published poet and a younger brother of the better-known writer Walter Savage Landor.

The porch of St Margaret's Church, 1868. On 26 and 27 December 1865, gentlemen of St Mary Magdalen College, Oxford (conducted by J. Stainer) gave two concerts in the Royal Assembly Rooms in Leamington to raise money for the enlargement and restoration of St Margaret's Church. The programmes included popular Christmas music and around £30 was raised. The following December, members of the Magdalen College Madrigal Society gave a concert in the Royal Pump Rooms and altogether sufficient money was raised to pay for the church porch. In recognition of this, a stone carving of a lily, the emblem of the college, was positioned above the door.

THE MAGDALEN PORCH.

A photograph of the trunk of the Whitnash Elm taken in the 1860s. It has been suggested by landscape historians that the presence of an aged pollard elm denotes an ancient settlement, for generations of suckers would have provided new trees when mature trees needed replacing.

Above: A wider view of the church and old tree, but some years later, for the churchyard is now surrounded by a stone wall, instead of a wooden fence. This view emphasises the fact that the elm was planted on the highest point of the church hill. Many have suggested that the first church building was deliberately situated on a site of pagan importance and the old elm may have been involved in the symbolism.

Right: The American writer Nathaniel Hawthorne visited Whitnash on several occasions between 1855 and 1860. Many of his observations were included in his book *Our Old Home*. Of the Whitnash Elm (which he thought was a yew) he wrote, 'The faces of two children laughed at us out of an opening in the trunk, which had become hollow with age'.

Above left: The two children in the hollow elm, in around 1910, are thought to be Daisy Young and Norma Wright who both lived close by. Obviously the tree was a playground for generations of local youngsters.

Above right: Thomas Hill of the Red Lion, Barford, *c*. 1890. He was related to the Masters family, members of whom were tenants of most of the farms in Whitnash during the first half of the twentieth century.

Left: Granny Masters, of Home Farm, photographed in the early twentieth century. The sheep was perhaps a pet.

Opposite: William Masters, gentleman farmer, *c*. 1907. Bill was one of Granny Masters' sons, and he farmed Green Farm for much of the first half of the twentieth century. In this photograph he is wearing cloth gaiters, but on his farm he often wore leather ones.

Church Lane as it was in the first half of the twentieth century. Historically this lane was part of an ancient road which led to Radford Semele. The wall on the right and the outbuildings of Manor Farm were demolished in the 1950s.

Members of the Masters family and their friends in the garden of Whitnash Manor House, *c.* 1910. Although the exterior was largely rendered at this time, the house possessed some impressive old beams, with part of the house dating back to the seventeenth century or before. George Masters, the tenant of Manor Farm, is on the right. The woman and baby on the left are believed to be visitors from London.

This view of Green Farm from the tower of St Margaret's Church was taken in the 1950s, but it could just as easily have been taken decades earlier. Behind the farmhouse and barn, Cooks Cottages can be seen and beyond them part of The Doglands is visible.

Green Farm in the early 1950s. The exterior of the house changed very little during the twentieth century. When he lived at Green Farm, Bill Masters used to keep canaries and budgerigars in the attic, and from the front windows of the house one could see horses being shod in the blacksmith's shop on the opposite side of the village green.

Landor's Cottages in Whitnash Road, with Grandma Watts on the left, Annie Watts in the centre and Mrs Kirby on the right, *c.* 1905. There were three cottages in the group and, prior to 1860, part of one was used as the village school. For much of the nineteenth and first part of the twentieth century, these cottages were owned by the Landor family, hence their name.

Whitnash Road, *c.* 1930. Brick-built cottages and the village bakery are on the left, whilst Landor's Cottages are on the right. Members of the Watts family still lived in the property at this time and eventually the name was changed to Watts Cottage.

Whitnash post office in Edwardian times. In the later nineteenth and the first few decades of the twentieth century, the post office and general store was situated in one of the first two dwellings of Cooks Cottages, and was run by members of the Heritage family. From the mid-twentieth century onwards, the post office was in Heathcote Road, first in Heathcote Terrace and later in one of the shops near Acre Close.

A group outside Whitnash bakery, *c.* 1903. The bakery store room was the building on the left, whilst to the right of the alley was the shop and living accommodation. The boy with the basket on the extreme left is Sam Ballard Watts, who eventually became the village baker. One woman appears to be holding a live chicken, which was perhaps a pet.

Home Farm in the mid-twentieth century. The house bears the date 1652 and it has been much praised by historians as a typical English farmhouse. For much of the nineteenth century it was owned by Henry Eyres Landor and a succession of relatively wealthy tenant-farmers were the occupiers. In the second half of the nineteenth century the Palmer family were the tenants, but by the late 1880s they seem to have fallen on hard times (perhaps losing money through the mismanagement by the two Greenway brothers of the Warwick bank of Greenway, Smith and Greenway in 1887, both of whom were jailed for dishonesty. Local councils and most local charities lost money as did many individuals) and they left Home Farm and moved into the smaller Homestead Farm, nearby. In the twentieth century, members of the Masters family became the tenants and in 1944 when the 200 acre farm was offered for sale, the tenant, Ernest Masters, bought it.

Opposite above: Home Farm stables and other outbuildings, *c.* 1910. Part of the charm of the farmhouse lay in the interesting and well-cared-for barns and animal pens. Although two of the barns were listed buildings, they were both demolished in the late 1950s, when most of the farm was sold for housing development.

Opposite below: Woodcarving in the drawing room of Home Farm in the 1920s. Two of the reception rooms in Home Farm had interesting carved over-mantels and fireplaces. It is possible that these were installed by Henry Eyres Landor, who, as a land agent, had opportunity to acquire reclaimed materials from upper-class clients who were rebuilding their houses.

The rear of St Margaret's Church from a Victorian painting. This image was taken from a New Year card sent in the early twentieth century. The railings near the East window of the church surround the graves of members of the Eyres family, who were the ancestors of the writer Walter Savage Landor and his brothers Henry Eyres Landor and Robert Eyres Landor.

The Golf House in 1909. The Leamington and County Golf Club bought land at Mollington Hill Farm and the course was opened in 1908. The road which gave access was then renamed Golf Lane.

The Barracks in the early years of the twentieth century. This row of thatched tenements, with the brick-built Holly Cottage on the right, was situated on the Leamington side of Whitnash School, and the wall of the playground can just be seen on the left. The Barracks were demolished in around 1939 and Holly Cottage some years later.

Cotterills' Cottage, near the Plough and Harrow public house in the 1950s. This dwelling was the home of several generations of the Cotterill family in the nineteenth and twentieth centuries. Generally considered to be the most attractive of all the cottage properties in the village, many were saddened when it was demolished in the late 1960s.

Cottages to the right of Cotterills' Cottage in the 1920s. Of the attractive group, only one now remains – the Vestry Cottage once inhabited by the Parish Clerk.

South Farm pond in the 1920s. The Vestry Cottages overlooked this picturesque pond, which was known locally as 'The Pit'. In all probability, the pond was spring-fed and when it was filled in during the late 1950s, water had to be diverted, via a culvert, to a nearby brook.

Haymaking near Osborne's Cottage in the 1930s. The man on the mower is Frank Roberts who later received the Agricultural Worker's Medal for long service on the land. The house still survives, although partially rebuilt, but the shops and houses of Home Farm Crescent now occupy the hayfield.

Above: The bride and groom are Sam and Emily Watts and their marriage took place in 1919, after Sam returned from service abroad during the First World War.

Left: Revd Claude A.H. Russell became Rector of Whitnash in 1919, succeeding his father Revd Alexander H.M. Russell, who had been Rector since 1884. Residents dressed an archway leading to the Rectory as a greeting on Claude Russell's arrival, but he only remained in Whitnash for four years.

This very rare snapshot, taken in the 1920s, shows part of Eskrick Cottage in the Heathcote Road, together with two smaller adjacent cottages. These cottages were demolished in the 1930s.

The Methodist chapel in Whitnash was erected in 1869 on a site adjoining that shown in the previous photograph. The waste ground to the right was once occupied by some half-timbered tenements, which were demolished in the 1930s. The chapel itself was demolished in 1959. In recent times, a great amount of earth has been removed from the site of the tenements and two houses have been built at road level.

Above: Farmer Bill Markham and his prize bull in the 1950s.

Left: Mrs Fox, flower and balloon seller, outside the National Provincial Bank on the corner of Dormer Place in Leamington, in the 1930s. She lived near Franklin Road in Whitnash and bought her flowers, often bronze spray-chrysanthemums, from Seekings' Nursery at the top of Golf Lane.

Above: Looking towards Glamis Cottage in 1938. The house on the left was called The Homestead and it still stands today, although much restored and renamed Elderfield. The old barn on the right belonged to Home Farm.

Right: Looking towards Home Farm in 1939. The two thatched houses adjoined the barn shown in the previous photograph.

The Boundary Oak in Tachbrook Road, opposite Ashford Road, is over 300 years old. Although sited in Whitnash, it is very close to the ancient boundary with Bishop's Tachbrook and is adjacent to the hawthorn hedge bordering the main road. The photograph was taken in 1992, but it could just as easily have been taken several decades earlier.

Marjorie Masters of Green Farm, in the garden of the Manor House, *c.* 1936. She later married Reg Marriott of Leamington and moved to Oxford.

The tower of St Margaret's Church in the 1930s. Dating from the late fifteenth century, the tower is the oldest part of the church as it was not rebuilt in Victorian times like the chancel and the nave. The tower may have been built by Benedict Medley, Lord of the Manor of Whitnash and Clerk of the Signet to King Henry VII, who died in 1503 and was buried in the chancel with his second wife, Agnes Govis. By the 1920s the old elm tree had been surrounded by stout metal railings.

Above: The area round the Plough and Harrow in the late 1930s. There are signs that change is imminent, for the field on the right is marked out in building plots. Between 1935 and 1939, there was ribbon development along both sides of Heathcote Road from the Plough to Heathcote Corner, and also along part of Whitnash Road from Halls Close to the Plough.

Left: Mrs Nellie Lines in her wedding dress in 1937. Typical of the new arrivals in the village, Mrs Lines moved into No. 68 Heathcote Road on her marriage. The cabbages in the foreground of this shot, which was taken in the back garden, seem to bear out the old saying that all brides look beautiful, whatever the surroundings.

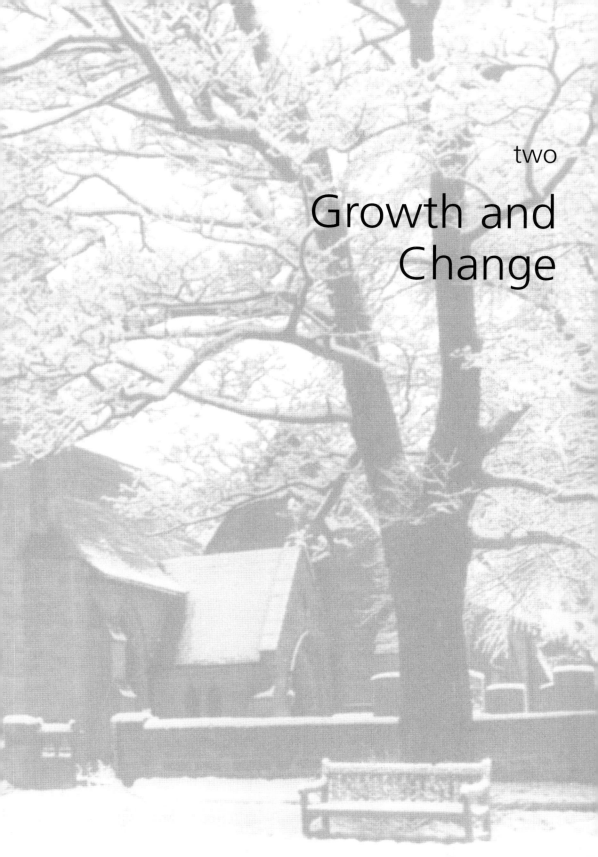

two

Growth and Change

The Whitnash Auxiliary Fire Service in 1941. The dignitary conducting the inspection is possibly the Duke of Kent. Second on the right is George Marlowe and the third is Jack Dolden. Both men lived in the Heathcote Road.

A parade of Sea Cadets in Beauchamp Avenue, Leamington Spa, *c.* 1943. On the extreme left is Lt-Com. Neal and the Mayor of Leamington carrying out the inspection is Councillor Salt. The cadet to whom the Mayor is speaking is Gerald Cox of Heathcote Road, Whitnash.

A services group outside St Margaret's Hall, *c.* 1941. From left to right, front row: Mr Jones, Mrs Bull, –?–, Mrs Pengelli, Betty Roberts, Sadie Clements, Dorothy Founge, Lilian George, Mrs Russell (Red Cross nurse), Mrs Cuthbert, Mrs Bodfish. Of the scouts on the right, the boy out of uniform is unknown, next is Bill George, Eric Davies, and Nigel Cuthbert on the extreme right. Second row of scouts: Derrick Seekings, Derek Butters, –?–, –?–. Mrs Jones (headmistress, in tilted black hat) and Francis Hubbard are behind Dorothy Founge. The second row of nurses are –?–, Mrs Cox, Mrs Lawrence, Marjorie Lawrence. Of the men at the back in the Auxiliary Fire Service, the front row is –?–, Tom Treadwell, Ted Masters, Frank Roberts, and Wilf Roberts. Steve Thornton is behind Ted Masters and next is Joe Evans, then Arthur Batchelor and Bob Hall. Of the other men, only the names of Victor Russell (behind Bob Hall) and Len Reading (top left) are known.

The Heathcote Inn in 1947. Completed in 1940, the building was used for military purposes during the Second World War. It opened as an inn in 1945 and since that time has been extended several times.

Green Farm on a winter's day, *c.* 1960.

The Heathcote Lane in 1947. 'The Sani Lane', as the road was often called, led past the Heathcote Sanitorium, an old isolation hospital for infectious diseases, which is just visible to the left, and on to Warwick, via Gallows Hill. Today, most of the trees are gone, the road has been widened, and housing development has taken place in the field to the left.

Dorothy Sumner at the Heathcote Inn, *c.* 1947. In the 1940s many women wore aprons and protected their hair with a scarf, worn turban style, when doing housework. The patterned woollen cardigan was typical of this era. From 1947-48, Dorothy and her husband John found accommodation at the Heathcote Inn, at a time when there was a great housing shortage.

Above: Visitors from Kent with their 1933
Lanchester outside the Heathcote Inn in
1947. The scattered buildings of the isolation
hospital can be seen, but in many ways the car
dominates the scene. Dorothy Sumner is on
the right.

Right: Revd Gleave, Rector of Whitnash,
inspects a striking piece of woodcarving in
1949. The carving had been completed by
Walter Summerton – the village carpenter in
Victorian times – on a large beam removed
from the belfry when repairs were carried out
to the tower of St Margaret's Church. The
carving formed part of an exhibition about
the history of Whitnash, which was held in
St Margaret's Hall.

Left: Davida Lines in the front garden of her parents' house in the Heathcote Road in 1950. Gnomes were then a popular feature in many gardens.

Below: The Prime Minister outside the New Hall, Heathcote Road in 1955. As part of the election campaign, Sir Anthony Eden, who had been MP for Warwick and Leamington since 1923, addressed a meeting in Whitnash, and later he signed autographs. He had become Prime Minister a few weeks before the election, on the resignation of Winston Churchill. His admirers are, from left to right: Carol Jacobs, Mrs Jacobs, Mrs Norman, Janice Norman, and Mrs Leech with baby Richard.

Above: Members of a Sunday School class on a seesaw near the New Hall, *c.* 1954. The children are, from left to right: Bobby Shakespeare, Geoffrey Benfield, Davida Lines, Carol Jacobs, Ray Benfield, -?-. The simple seesaw was one the first pieces of play equipment to be installed in Whitnash.

Right: John Sumner, with son Philip, pauses in the front garden of No. 108 Heathcote Road in 1951. The light sportscoat and dark trousers were typical mens wear at the time.

Left: Jackie Armstrong with son Gregory in the pram inspecting progress on their new house, then under construction in Summerton Road, in February 1953.

Below: Young and old, on an allotment near the present site of Acre Close, *c.* 1953. Davida Lines is the girl on the left, but the names of the others are not known. There had been allotments on that site since 1905.

Opposite above: Philip Sumner and his younger brother Peter, with their grandmother Mrs Rosa Sumner, in the front porch of her house in the Heathcote Road, *c.* 1957. Standing behind is an aunt, who was visiting from Perth, Western Australia. Philip's elastic belt, with its distinctive snake-shaped fastening, was popular wear for boys for several decades.

John, Richard and Jeremy Hunt in 1949. As Whitnash was considered a relatively safe area, Mrs Hunt and her eldest son lodged in the Heathcote Road for a time during the Second World War while Mr Hunt was in the forces. When the family moved back down south, regular visits were paid to their wartime home.

The Whitnash Elm · March 31st 1959
breaking its buds probably for the 1000th time
Trunk Girth nearly 30 feet

Above: A photograph showing a very different looking village green, *c.* 1961. This is one of a series of postcards produced by the Midland View Company of Market Harborough.

Opposite above: This watercolour by H.W. Box shows the Whitnash Elm in March 1959. Whether it was the thousandth time the tree had broken its buds was never established, but it was certainly the last, for the tree was removed by order of the Parish Council, in January 1960. A vigorous campaign was mounted to try to save the tree and the story was carried by Midlands television newsreels as well as many national newspapers, but all to no avail. Some estimates put the girth of the trunk at 36ft.

Opposite below: The village green seen in deep shadow, *c.* 1955. The diagonal path across to the Manor Farm and Church Lane was soon to disappear.

The former Homestead farmhouse, latterly the home of the farmer Tad (Edward) Palmer, was re-roofed and extensively renovated in 1959. Tad, together with Bob, his faithful sheepdog, was forced to live out his days in lodgings in Leamington, whilst a new section of road was constructed where one of his fields had been. The dwelling was renamed Elderfield.

Whitnash Manor House awaiting demolition, c. 1959. Wooden beams were exposed in the oldest section of the house, and in the once beautiful garden only the elegant steps remained intact.

Two seventeenth-century cottages in Whitnash Road, although apparently in good repair look rather forlorn, c. 1960. Eventually a bungalow was built on the site to the left, and the cottages, having been turned into one, were renovated. Today, the cottage garden is well tended and Lupin Cottage, as it has been named, is a period property of considerable charm.

The Doglands, c. 1959. Of all the old properties in Whitnash in this era of change, this perhaps fared best. Newly thatched and painted, the dwellings still possessed a traditional cottage garden.

Heathcote Road in around 1961 – another card by the Midland View Company.

Acre Close shops, c. 1961. This view was taken by the same firm, a few hundred yards down the road from the viewpoint in the previous photograph. The shops are much as they are today, with the post office and general store second on the left.

Floods near the Plough and Harrow in autumn 1966. The building on the right was a bottle store, but being cool it was also used from time to time as a mortuary in the nineteenth and early twentieth centuries. Inquests were sometimes held in the Plough and Harrow.

The Women's Institute hut stood next to the Plough and Harrow car park. Opened in 1936, it was used for a variety of public meetings until its demolition in around 1983.

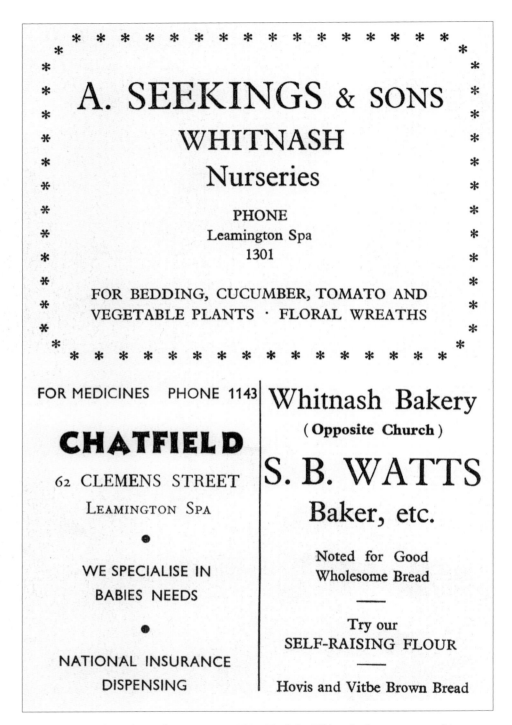

A. SEEKINGS & SONS

WHITNASH

Nurseries

PHONE
Leamington Spa
1301

FOR BEDDING, CUCUMBER, TOMATO AND
VEGETABLE PLANTS · FLORAL WREATHS

FOR MEDICINES   PHONE 1143

CHATFIELD

62 CLEMENS STREET

LEAMINGTON SPA

●

WE SPECIALISE IN
BABIES NEEDS

●

NATIONAL INSURANCE
DISPENSING

Whitnash Bakery

(Opposite Church)

S. B. WATTS

Baker, etc.

Noted for Good
Wholesome Bread

——

Try our
SELF-RAISING FLOUR

——

Hovis and Vitbe Brown Bread

A page from a Whitnash Parish Magazine in 1951. Until the Whitnash pharmacy opened in around 1961, Chatfield was one of the nearest chemists. The Whitnash bakery closed in the late 1950s but Seekings' nursery did not close until 1985.

St Margaret's Church choir, *c.* 1965. The Rector, the Revd Gleave, is on the left, with Mr Pratt, organist and choirmaster, next to him. The older choristers are, from left to right: Brian Burrows, Ian Box, Revd Lewis (Curate), Ian Kennedy (in front of Revd Lewis) Mr Bailey, Raymond King, Mr Runchman and Revd Mallet.

Green Arrow, No. 4771, approaches Black Bridge from the south in the mid-1970s. The banks of the railway in Whitnash have long afforded good vantage points from which to observe or photograph trains. Some photographers prefer the background of Whitnash cutting, whilst others, like Bill Armstrong in this shot, prefer to include Black Bridge.

A sketch of two elm trees by H.W. Box in the mid–1950s. To people walking along the Heathcote Road, these trees, situated behind Tabor's Dairy and Avon Road, appeared to form the silhouette of a lion. There were numerous beautiful elm trees in the village, until they were killed off by Dutch elm disease.

A rare photograph of the meadow and pond, near the rear of Home Farm in the mid-1950s. Today the site is occupied by the houses in Palmer Road.

Home Farm in around 1961, as photographed by the Midland View Company. The magnificent half-timbered farmhouse, devoid of outbuildings, looks almost out of place surrounded by modern houses and bungalows.

Whitnash Road, *c.* 1961. This postcard, issued by the same company, complements the view of Home Farm. The walls round the garden of the farmhouse can be seen to the left, and bungalows occupy the site of the former barn. Further down the road, Watts Cottage and Green Farm remain unchanged.

The view to the north-east from St Margaret's Church tower, *c.* 1957. By 1967 many of the houses in Greville Smith Avenue had been built on the former Manor House farm, but a decade earlier the scene was vastly different. The branches in the foreground are those of the large cedar at the side of the church. The roof of the farm buildings is in the centre and amongst the trees is a caravan belonging to Mr Greenhalgh. In the distance are the fields leading to the brook and Radford Semele.

The church and green on a winter's day in the 1960s. The presence of snow seems to enhance views such as this and since amateur photographers have rushed to record the scene, many similar photographs exist.

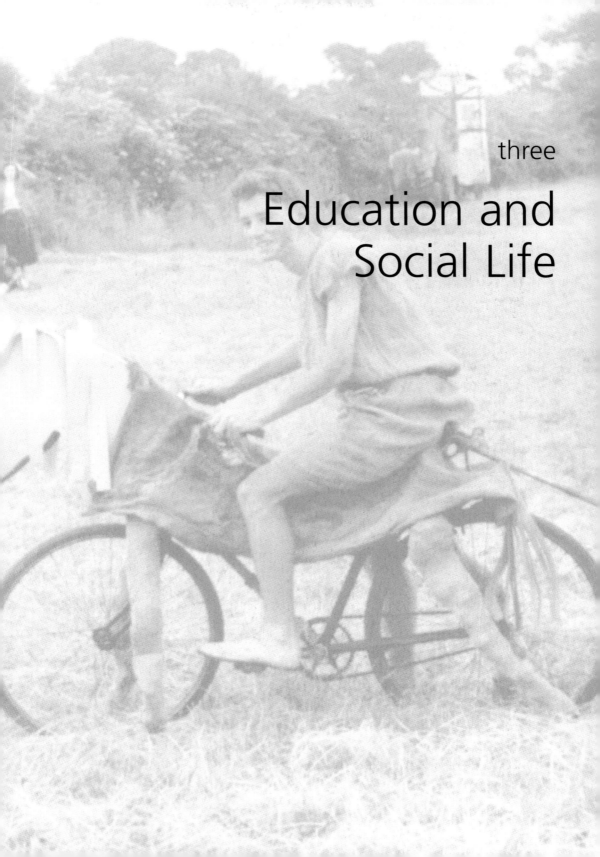

three

Education and Social Life

Whitnash schoolchildren stand outside the village school, *c.* 1907. The school was built in 1860 at the expense of Henry Eyres Landor, who donated the site and also left a substantial endowment for its upkeep. Now part of St Margaret's Church Centre, the school buildings and the schoolhouse remain little altered today.

May Day procession from Whitnash School to the village green, *c.* 1930. The celebrations appear to have been organised annually by Whitnash School during the second or third week in May. A king and queen were chosen from the younger children, and a pram chassis, suitably decorated, appears to have been used as a royal carriage. A pole, garlanded with flowers, was carried by one of the older boys.

A fancy dress party at the Rectory, *c.* 1937. From left to right, back row: Mrs Edwards, –?–, Gordon Dingley, Vilma Avis, Yvonne Avis. Second row: Pam Edwards, Iris Summers, Frances Hubbard, Lilian George, Mrs Slin. Third row: Pat Dingley, –?–, –?–, –?–, Terry Percox. Of those on the front row, only Cecily Summers on the extreme right is known.

Mrs Daisy Nichols (centre), the long-serving teacher of the Infants class at Whitnash Endowed (Church of England) School is being presented with flowers and a handbag in St Margaret's Hall during the 1940s, perhaps to commemorate an anniversary. Mrs Jones, the headmistress, is on the left, and the Revd Gleave, Rector of Whitnash, is on the right.

May Day celebrations in Whitnash on Friday 22 May 1936. Several different photographs exist of this particular celebration, one being included in the *Leamington Spa Courier*. Eight of the older girls shown here gave a dancing display with ribbons round a maypole, which was erected in the centre of the green.

Whitnash Carnival in 1950. 'Ancient Britons on Tour' with Mick Marlowe (left) and Neil Harkness was one of the entries in the cycle class of the fancy dress competition.

In the playing field outside the New Hall, Mick Marlowe and Neil Harkness receive a prize for their entry. Included in the photograph are, from left to right: Percy G. Smith, Audrey Clarke, Pat Risdale (Miss Whitnash), Flo Place and Mrs Martin.

In 1949 the Whitnash Mothers' Union, plus the children of some members, mimed the biblical quotation, 'By the waters of Babylon we sat down and wept'. A series of tableaux from MU groups in the diocese took place in the Urquhart Hall in Leamington. From right to left are Mrs Russell, Ann Trindall and Mrs Hall, but the names of the other women are not known. The two young people in the front are David Hewins and Jean Addicott.

Flo Place and Ken Wakefield in *The Girl in Question* performed by the Whitnash Players in 1947. It seems a difficult feat to create an aura of glamour amid rather rickety scenery in a church hall, but this couple seemed to have managed admirably. The Whitnash Players first performed in a gaslit St Margaret's Hall in 1945, with the electric stage lights being run from the nearby cowshed in Green Farm.

The Pied Piper of Hamelin was performed by pupils of Whitnash School, *c.* 1954. From left to right, back row: Douglas Edwards, Jean Golligher, Gillian Herbert, Linda Taylor, –?–, Dorothy Frost. Middle row: Annette Pavier, Judith Davies, Jane Haslam, Ian Box, Geoffrey Ashton, –?–. Front group: Raymond Greenhalgh, –?–, Pat Symes, Robert Ayres (behind Pat), Rosemary Warren, Jean Billington (cat with crown), Alan Masters, Pauline Gray, Roy Hadfield (with ruff), Geoffrey Benfield, Christine Partland.

This playlet by Whitnash School pupils in around 1955 had a strong animal theme. From left to right, back row: Derek Owen, –?–, Alan Masters, Pat Symes, –?–, Ian Box, –?–. Front row: Roy Hadfield, –?–, Gordon Franklin, –?–, Robert Ayres.

One of the first New Year parties provided for the Darby and Joan Club in the early 1950s. Third on the right is Mrs Symes, seventh is Mrs Robbins, while Mrs Hemmings is sixth on the left. Mrs Dolden is standing on the extreme right.

This Darby and Joan New Year Party was held in the Women's Institute on 25 January 1953.

The Whitnash football team of 1959. From left to right, back row: Bill Ward, Colin Lishman, Les Clarkson, -?-, Bruce Black, -?-. Only Des Harrison on the extreme left is known of those players in the front row.

The Whitnash football team of 1961. From left to right, back row: Frank Mitchell, Mick Raven, Mick O'Grady, -?-, Les Clarkson, Geoff Bott, Mike Joynes. Front row: -?-, David Owen, Ken Walters, Roger Saveker, Derek Owen.

The bowls section of Whitnash Sports and Social Club was formed in 1962. In the earliest days only men were allowed to play. From left to right: Eric Perkins, Ralph Taylor, Harry Fisher, Ernie Owen, Eric Morris (back), Alec Wood, -?-, Alec Ibbotson. Of the three men in the doorway only Jack Wykes (middle) is known.

In 1962 the wives of bowlers were expected to watch their menfolk or make the tea. Watching in a chilly wind are: -?-, Sybil Taylor, Sadie Taylor, Irene Ibbotson and Eva Yarwood. Happily this state of affairs did not continue for long and soon there was a flourishing women's bowling section.

A meeting of older residents in the Women's Institute in the early 1960s. Mr Lancaster, an ex-railway guard who once worked on the Royal Train, is third from the left and the Rector, Revd Gleave, is on the centre. Frank Roberts is on the extreme right and Mrs Eden of Heathcote Road stands in the doorway to the kitchen.

The cast of *Mountain Air* as performed by the Whitnash Players in the New Hall in 1952. From left to right, back row: Derrick Seekings, Alec Templeton, Bert Seekings, Des Davies, Tom Commander. Front row: Eva Orange, Mary Boneham, Flo Place.

Right: Mr and Mrs Frank Roberts on their Golden Wedding Anniversary in the 1980s. Frank had previously been awarded an Agricultural Worker's Medal for working on the land for fifty years.

Below: Sam Ballard Watts, the former village baker, is on the left of this group, with Mr Green in the centre and Mr Hughes on the right. The function was probably a party for older residents in around 1960.

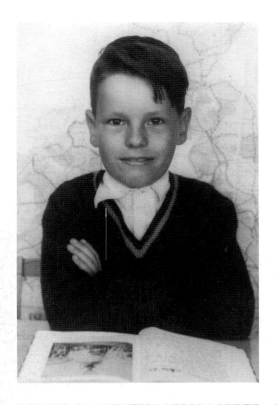

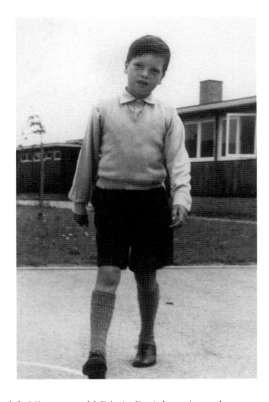

Above left: Nine-year-old Edwin Pettipher, pictured here in 1958, was one of the first pupils at Whitnash Combined School in Langley Road, which opened in 1956.

Above right: Paul Pettipher, aged seven, is photographed here in 1959 against a background of some of the early school buildings.

Left: Judith Ann Pettipher (now Falp) photographed at Whitnash Combined School in 1962. At the age of eight she already had the confident air of a future Mayor of Whitnash and District Councillor.

A group of Brownies in St Margaret's Hall, *c*. 1961. Heather Kennedy is at the back on the left, with Snowy Owl, Jean Billington, immediately in front of her. On the right at the back is Pam Horley, with Ann Merrick in front of her. St Margaret's Hall was built in 1922 and until the late 1960s it was used for a wide variety of meetings. Between 1922 and 1936, when the Women's Institute opened, it was the only hall in the village.

Above: David and Gregory Armstrong on the footbridge over the Whitnash Brook in the 1960s. The old willows, planted in the nineteenth century for osier production, make a grotesque-looking background. Farm records from around 1900 refer to the harvesting of withy tops. The footpath to Radford Semele which crosses the footbridge has been popular with walkers for centuries.

Left: Jackie Armstrong (later Warmington) at a Tramps Evening organised for the Whitnash Youth Club in the New Hall, *c*. 1965.

Opposite above: Miss Whitnash leads the carnival procession to Acre Close playing fields, *c*. 1970. Leslie Burrows is the man in the check cap to the right.

Opposite below: This group of Brownies, with Jean Clarkson, Brown Owl, as Snow White, took part in the Whitnash Carnival of 1974. Linda Owen is at the back near Snow White.

Above: St Margaret's Junior School in the late 1960s. In the centre of this group of older pupils are, from left to right: Mr Runchman, Mrs Bateman Jones (retired headmistress) and Mr Jones, the headmaster. The name of the other adult is not known. Nigel Sibley is on the extreme right in the front row, and Susan Draper is on the left in the middle row. Paul Riley is second from the left in the back row, Victoria Bland is fifth and Jane White is thirteenth.

Left: Dorothy Burrows and Tom Shakespeare in a play rehearsal. *A Quiet Weekend* was produced by the Whitnash Players in autumn 1965.

The hall of St Margaret's Church of England School in 1971. A group of young bell ringers, clad in medieval costume, ring tunes on the hand bells, under the watchful eye of Percy Oram, Tower Captain. Wearing a monk's habit, Mr Oram is on the right. From left to right, the ringers are Wendy Grimwood, Christina Broady, Val Higgins, Susan Kennedy, Carol Roberts, Robert Fletcher and Anthony Davies. To the left of Wendy Grimwood is Peter Wilson.

The Avon Road Jubilee Party in 1977. From left to right, on the raised back row: Sheila Kirton, Gill Barker, Ian Barker. The adults and taller youngsters in the front row are Julie Higham as the Queen, Teresa Adamson, -?-, -?-, -?-, -?-, Bernard Kirton, -?-, -?-, and Mark Kirton as a sea captain. The young children in the front row are Duncan Smith (standing forward) Gary Whitlock, Scott Whitlock, Lee Smith, Jenny Smith, Joanne Tighe, Martin Higham as Mrs Mop, -?-, Joe Mulleague (half-hidden, arm raised) and Mark Buswell with the flag.

A group of Brownies pose outside Old Whitnash School in 1988 to celebrate Jean Clarkson's twenty-five years as Brown Owl. From left to right, back row: Linda Draper, -?-, Jane White, Deidre Hayward, Carol Kennedy, -?-, -?-, -?-, Mrs Brogan, -?-, Mrs Payne, Alison Payne, Jane Crutchington, Jane Hemming, Lynn Wyatt and Olive Billington.

The twenty-eighth anniversary of the Darby and Joan Club in 1978. The three women at the front, by the tree, are Ethel Bedford (left), Betty Stephens (centre), and Group Leader Jean Holmes (nearest the camera). Mrs Tew (wearing a triple-strand necklace) is in the centre of the group, and Mr Simmonds is at the back on the right. Mr and Mrs Tew lived in Whitnash Road for many years and were very well known in the area. The Darby and Joan Club was set up in 1950 by the Women's Voluntary Service and it was very popular for over fifty years. However, at the end of 2004, when club leaders Phyllis and Clive Hodgkins decided to retire after eighteen years in charge, the club was officially closed.

Right: The Queen's Guide Award was presented to Jackie Jones and Sarah Devey in March 1983. Guide Commissioner, Carolyn Chatwin, made the presentation in St Margaret's Church Centre.

Below: A May-time festival at St Margaret's School in 1974. From left to right, front row: Vanessa Gossage, Jill Cochrane, Sharon Fenn. Back row: Nancy Ellis, Tracey Grimwood, Sue Stocks, -?-. Queen of the May is eleven-year-old Jacqueline Syms, who was chosen by the whole school.

The much-respected John Handford, headmaster of Oken School in Warwick from its opening in 1954 to his retirement in 1968.

The Women's British Isles Bowling Championships in June 1980. Over a hundred members of the International teams of England, Ireland, Scotland and Wales took part in these championships which were staged at Whitnash Bowling Club.

Campion School speech day in July 1982. From left to right, back row: Ricky Thorpe Smith (deputy head) Mollie Roberts (headteacher), Hilary Laud (now Hampton, deputy head), Richard Taylor (deputy head). Front row: Roy Charles (Mayor of Leamington), Fiona Morris (head girl), John Higgins (Chairman of the District Council), Robert Bowyer (head boy).

Left: Whitnash resident, teacher John Britton, on his retirement from Myton School, Warwick in 1986. Myton School was formed by an amalgamation of Oken and Beauchamp High Schools in 1968. Over the decades many Whitnash youngsters attended the secondary schools on the Myton Road site. Mr Britton is pictured with some third year pupils.

Mollie Roberts, headteacher of Campion School in Leamington, shows her OBE to the local press and some older school pupils in 1984. The honour was announced on 31 December 1983, the citation being 'for services to education'. Yorkshire-born, Mrs Roberts had been headteacher of Campion School for Girls in Leicester Street, and in September 1973, when the Campion Boys' and Girls' Schools merged on a new site at Sydenham, she was appointed headteacher of the new comprehensive. Over the years many pupils from Whitnash have attended Campion School, the grounds of which adjoin the Whitnash boundary.

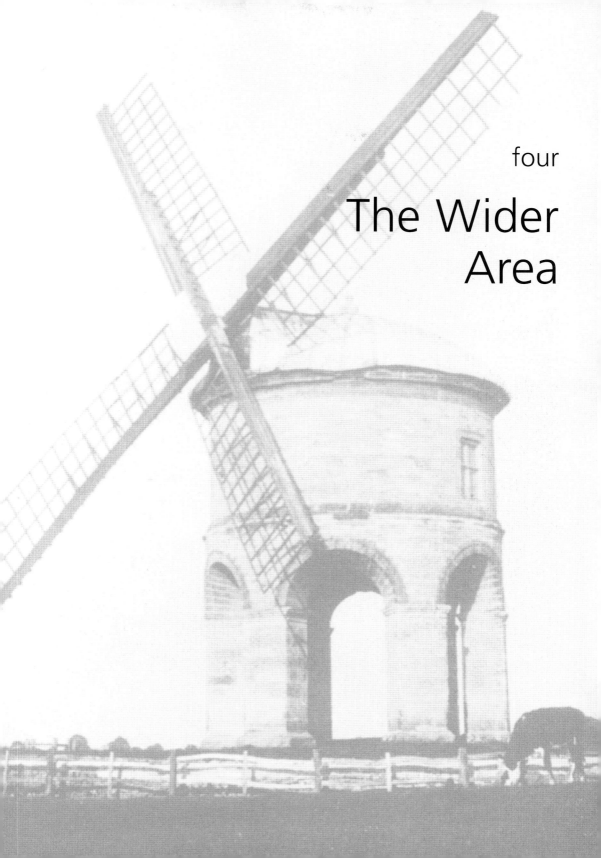

four

The Wider Area

Leamington Parish Church and old cottages in 1822. Although Leamington had begun to grow rapidly, there still remained a few older dwellings reminiscent of village life. Today, only a couple of such cottages remain and these are no longer thatched.

Leamington Parade in 1847. Apart from the absence of the present Town Hall, and the fact that Christchurch occupied a prominent position in Clarendon Square, the scene is not that different today.

Savage's House in Bishop's Tachbrook in the mid-nineteenth century. Henry Eyres Landor, Lord of the Manor of Whitnash, and later his nieces, lived in the old Tachbrook Manor House from 1840-92. For several centuries previously, the house had been in the possession of the Savage family and it had been the childhood home of Henry's mother, Elizabeth Savage.

St Chad's Church, Bishop's Tachbrook, in the mid-nineteenth century. Henry Eyres Landor and his nieces, Sophy and Kitty, were buried in the churchyard, all three in the same grave. Henry died in 1866, Sophy in 1889 and Kitty in 1892. The property with the thatched roof was the New Inn.

Above: This heart-shaped motif is part of a mosaic discovered during excavations of the site of a Roman villa in the parish of Chesterton. The southern boundary of Whitnash is formed by the Roman Fosse Way and recent archaeological research indicates that another Roman road may have crossed the fields of Whitnash from the site of a Roman villa at nearby Radford Semele.

Left: Chesterton Windmill in the 1930s. The distinctive structure was erected in 1632 from a design attributed to Inigo Jones and, until motor traffic made the roads difficult for pedestrians, it was a popular destination for a walk and picnic. From the mill, there is a marvellous view of Highdown Wood and the surrounding country.

Right: Chesterton Windmill undergoing restoration. Work commenced in 1966 and was completed in 1971. 'The design of the mill is unique both structurally and mechanically', claims the information board now erected for the benefit of visitors. It is still possible to walk to the mill along a path through a cultivated field, and occasionally the public have the opportunity to see the sails turning and flour being ground.

Below: Chesterton Mill House in the 1930s. The old stone house appeared to be almost derelict for many years and it fascinated those who knew of its existence for they imagined a romantic history. To many it seemed that the Mill House was in keeping with the eerie atmosphere that seemed to pervade the tiny village of Chesterton. The house, which was built in around 1660, was restored some years ago, the owners now restricting access to the watermill and pool.

The road to Warwick from the south in the early nineteenth century. To many people from Whitnash, this view would have been very familiar as they walked the three miles into the county town.

Northgate (right) and Northgate House, Warwick, in 1951. This pair of elegant houses is said to stand, more or less, on the site of the North Gate of Warwick, which had been demolished by the early 1500s. The houses were apparently built in the late 1600s, for the date 1698 appears on a rainwater head. In around 1830, Henry Eyres Landor, who became Lord of the Manor of Whitnash in 1826, was living and running his legal practice in Northgate, which was conveniently close to his sisters and his mother, then living in Landor House, Smith Street.

Above: A group of girl guides from Leamington visit Warwick Workhouse, *c.* 1925. Situated on what is now part of Warwick Hospital, this Union Workhouse (closed in the early 1930s) served not only the town of Warwick but also numerous villages, one of them being Whitnash. Pictured with Mr and Mrs Measures, the last Master and Mistress of the Workhouse, are, from left to right: Kathleen Sharp, -?-, -?-, Joan Bromwich and Guide Captain Miss Markwick. The front row is Bessie Clark, -?-, and Kathleen Thorpe.

Right: Max Miller on the stage of the Coventry Theatre in 1936. From the 1920s onwards, coach trips to theatres in Coventry or Stratford were organised from Whitnash as special outings.

Maypole dancing in the grounds of Shrubland Hall in 1916. The large house, the home of the influential Wise family, was situated around a quarter of a mile off the Tachbrook Road in Leamington, on the Warwick side of Baker Avenue. In the nineteenth century, before St John's Church was built, the Wise family had many connections with St Margaret's at Whitnash.

A thatched cottage near to the Manor House in Radford Semele in 1950. The cottage stills survives today although somewhat altered in appearance.

The billiard team of St Mark's in Leamington, *c.* 1925. From left to right, back row: Lawson, Jenkins, Heath, Caldicott, Churmage. Front row: Walker, Box, Vincent. W. Churmage, the scorer, who perhaps lost an arm in the First World War, sold cleaning materials, door to door, round Whitnash and other villages, from a large pram body, which he fitted with lift-up lids, from the 1920s until the 1940s.

The members of St Mark's Sunday school walking to the annual service in the Parish Church in Leamington, *c.* 1930. The photograph was taken in Binswood Street and the scene is instantly recognisable today, except that a large traffic island occupies the centre of the road junction and the buildings on the extreme left have been demolished.

Left: Alice Willis and her stepson Tom outside their home in Bishop's Tachbrook in the 1920s. On the back of the photograph the address is given as No. 91 The Knob. The decorative rail above the window was similar in style to Cotterill's Cottage in Whitnash.

Below: The Lockheed Orchestra at the time of a broadcast for *Workers' Playtime* in the 1940s. As it was situated just over the Whitnash boundary, many Whitnash people worked at the car-components factory, especially from the 1940s to the 1980s. George Marlowe is the trumpet player on the right, and Margaret Marlowe, a well-known teacher of stringed instruments, is the first violinist on the left.

five

Flavels
(Rangemaster)

The original site of the Eagle Foundry in 1856. Although John Flavel began the firm in Bilton, near Rugby in 1777, it was his son, William, who came to Leamington in 1803 and laid the foundations of the successful firm. William Flavel made numerous inventions, including a closed cooking range, which he called a kitchener, in 1829. Soon new premises were needed and in 1833 a site adjacent to the canal was purchased, near Brunswick Street. The Rangemaster (Flavels) factory still occupies this site, although various expansions have taken place over the years.

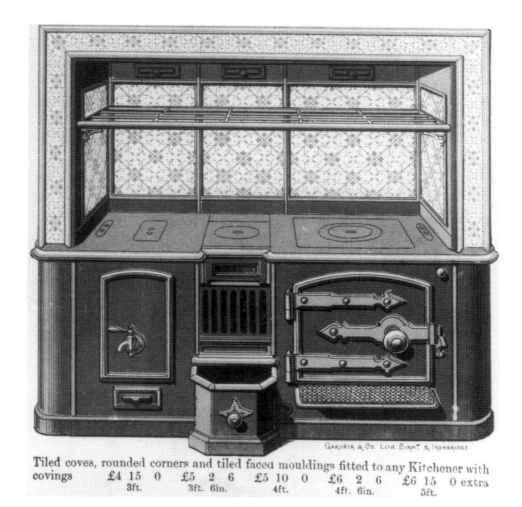

Tiled coves, rounded corners and tiled faced mouldings fitted to any Kitchener with
covings   £4 15 0   £5 2 6   £5 10 0   £6 2 6   £6 15 0 extra
      3ft.   3ft. 6in.   4ft.   4ft. 6in.   5ft.

Above: A Flavels kitchener, *c.* 1850. William Flavel died in 1844, but his son Sidney carried on the
business and, after exhibiting in London at the Great Exhibition of 1851, the orders rolled in.
Many variations of the original model were possible in sizes from 3ft to 8ft wide. Soon the client
list included Queen Victoria and other royal families in Europe, and models were being sent all
over the world, including a number to Australia.

Opposite below: The Eagle site as drawn by Hanslip Fletcher in early 1925. In 1902 Flavels had
bought out The Imperial Stove Company, a rival firm set up by two ex-employees, whose
foundry was The Imperial Works (now Fords) in Leamington. By the early 1920s both sites
needed refurbishment and modernisation, following the making of products for the Government
from 1914-18. Before any rebuilding took place, the well-known artist was called in to record
the old buildings on the Eagle site, many of which had been built in 1887, when kitchener sales
were at their height. As regards the transport of raw materials and finished products, both Eagle
and Imperial were very well placed, for both were very close to the railway, which provided
opportunity for special sidings and also advertisements which could be read by rail passengers.
Eagle also adjoined the canal, which fact was very important, especially in the early days.

Left: A gas cooker of 1902. Sales of kitcheners diminished in the twentieth century as gas cookers and gas fires began to take their place as the most popular products. The early gas cookers had the gas taps on the side and were still made from wrought and cast iron.

Below: During the depression years of the 1920s and '30s a variety of products were tried, including this free-standing, coal-burning Victor stove.

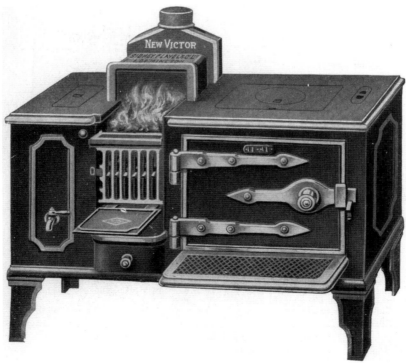

Perhaps the best known of all the Flavel family was Sidney Flavel Jnr (1847-1931) who was educated at Warwick School, and later became a Freeman of the borough in addition to becoming Mayor of Leamington six times. In his later years he lived in Bushbury Lodge in the Willes Road, which was relatively close to the foundry. He proved an excellent life-chairman of the firm, which by this time had been incorporated.

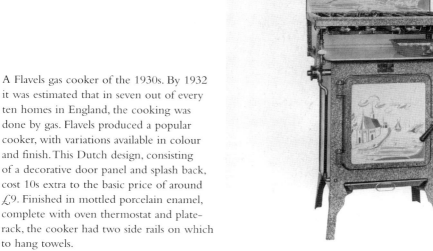

A Flavels gas cooker of the 1930s. By 1932 it was estimated that in seven out of every ten homes in England, the cooking was done by gas. Flavels produced a popular cooker, with variations available in colour and finish. This Dutch design, consisting of a decorative door panel and splash back, cost 10s extra to the basic price of around £9. Finished in mottled porcelain enamel, complete with oven thermostat and plate-rack, the cooker had two side rails on which to hang towels.

Above: Digging the foundations for an extension to the Imperial Foundry, 10 September 1923. Princes Drive had only recently been completed and the foundry had all the appearance of being on a greenfield site. The site of the extension had formerly been allotments and first the remains of cabbages and other crops had to be cleared. A variety of horses and carts were used to assist the contractors and much of the work was done by hand.

Left: The Eagle Foundry, 16 September 1925. The large notice, which once stood proudly above the entrance of the Victorian foundry, is on the point of being taken down, ready to make way for new premises in which to manufacture more modern appliances.

Opposite: Demolition at the Eagle Foundry on 25 September 1925, from the opposite viewpoint to that in the previous photograph. The famous entrance has now gone and the houses opposite in Clarence Street are clearly visible. Extremely long wooden ladders, with thirty-two or more rungs, are being used, the workers having little or no protective headgear or special clothing.

Left: An advertisement for a Flavel gas-panel heater in the 1930s. During the depression years all firms were forced to try harder to produce quality wares with unusual selling points, and these attractive heaters looked very modern for their day. Available in a range of colours and models, suitable for all rooms of the house, some could be recessed into a wall to save space.

Below: A reproduction fireplace produced by Flavels in the 1920s and '30s. Not only did Flavels manufacture the metal grate, but they also supplied the fire surround, fire irons and other sundries. By the late '30s trade was sometimes slack, but the outbreak of the Second World War in 1939 provided the opportunity of Government work. Ammunition boxes were reconditioned and a number of other Government contracts were obtained, for Flavels possessed some extremely large presses able to assist with the manufacture of numerous steel items.

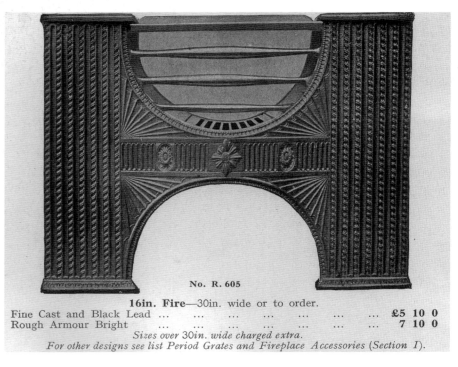

No. R. 605

16in. Fire—30in. wide or to order.

Fine Cast and Black Lead ...	...	...	...	...	...	...	**£5 10 0**
Rough Armour Bright	...	...	...	...	...	...	**7 10 0**

Sizes over 30in. wide charged extra.
For other designs see list Period Grates and Fireplace Accessories (Section I).

The Flavels Christmas party for children in 1943. Held in the wartime canteen, at the suggestion of Mrs Isobel Flavel, then Chairman of the Board, this was the first such party in modern times. From left to right, back row: Len Harbour, Peggy Harris, Nurse Roberts, Mrs Flavel, nine girls from St Ann's Home in Leamington, a party entertainer, Bill Box, and Teddy Roberts, the foundry manager, on the far right. The second row is made up of five mistresses from the home, plus Mrs Roberts who is in front of the entertainer. Director Duncan Wright is on the left of the group of younger children and Freddy Rogers is on the right. The author, aged five, in a dress with a white collar, is sitting next to Freddy Rogers.

Some long-serving employees of Flavels on 11 December 1952. Those with twenty-five-years service and more were presented with a clock at a function at Chesford Grange Hotel to mark the 175th anniversary of the firm. From left to right: W. Seaton, E. Boyle, F. Hammond, -?-, H.W. Box, G. Essex, E. Roberts, W. Brookes, F. Willman, F. Healey, J. Redgrave, F. Watts, P.J. Hammond, G. King, S. Francis, E.H. Goode, A.R. Cleaver, A. Willoughby, W.J. Parsons, O.R. Toone. Other long-serving employees not in this photograph included Mr F.G. Aitkin, Mr E.R. Bartlett, Mr W. Bister, Mr J. Dumbleton, Mr J. Locke, Miss G.L. MacLaren, Mr W. Parkes, Mr H. Ward, Mr B.G. Watkins, Miss M. Womersley.

Opposite above: Some of the guests at the Chesford Grange reception in 1952. From left to right, back row: John Taylor, Sam Lake, -?-, George Aitkin, Gladys Horne, Sab Sabin. Seated: Doll Bromley, George Nichols, Snowy Houghton.

Opposite below: The visit of local MP Anthony Eden to help promote the new '68' gas cooker in 1950. From left to right are Arnold Jackson, Anthony Eden, Jack Allen, Fred Rogers and Duncan Wright. After the Second World War production of gas cookers and gas fires of various types was stepped up because of the number of houses being built to replace those damaged in the war. Flavels secured a number of contracts from local gas boards and large numbers of cookers and fires were ordered.

Left: The bestselling Flavel Debonair gas fire, the first to have a wooden surround in various finishes, began production in 1961. Many new homes with no fireplace had a Debonair, with a light wood surround, on a focal wall in the lounge, but places such as hotels, with wood-panelled walls and large traditional fireplaces also found that a fire with a dark wood surround did not look out of place. In the end, well over half a million Debonair fires were produced, and a public house near the factory, and even a cocktail, was named after it.

Below: A Press Shop outing to Southend in 1953. Social events were encouraged so that a family atmosphere was built up, which in turn brought a great sense of loyalty amongst the workers. Over a long period Flavels seem to have been very successful in retaining their highly skilled staff.

A winning stand by Flavels Horticultural Society at Leamington Flower Show, *c.* 1950. With garden produce grown by the members, the comprehensive display of vegetables, fruit and flowers made an impressive exhibit. The Horticultural Society had been formed in 1940 as part of the Dig for Victory campaign during the Second World War and the first chairman was Arnold Jackson, with Bill Box as the first secretary. The Horticultural Society was one of the sections of the Flavel Social and Athletic Club, other sections included darts, dominoes, football, cricket, swimming, snooker, table tennis, photography, badminton, angling, boxing and athletics. Each year the Flavels Flower Show was held by the Horticultural Society, either in the canteen or on the nearby Eagle Recreation Ground, but after the fiftieth show in 1990, the Horticultural Society was discontinued.

The Flavel Bicentenary Queen in 1977. Angie Case, with Maids of Honour Pam Hawkins and Kay Robinson, helped the firm to celebrate their 200 years of history. A reception was held at Stoneleigh and employees were given a leaflet outlining the firm's history and a commemorative ashtray.

Whitnash resident Margaret Lucas and Chief Accountant Robin Coleman in 1990. Having worked in the Accounts Department for nearly thirty years, Mrs Lucas was given a good send-off by her colleagues. She was the second generation of her family to work for Flavels, as her mother, Margaret Webster, had worked in the Porcelain Enamel Department for ten years in the 1940s. A one-time Secretary of the Horticultural Society, Mrs Lucas later joined the committee of Flavels Retirement Club. She first moved to Whitnash in 1952.

The kitchener patented by William Flavel in 1829, as manufactured on the Eagle site from 1833. Since Flavels made their name producing kitchen ranges, it seems entirely appropriate that during the 1990s the bestselling product was once again a substantial kitchen range. The Flavels name has since been dropped in favour of Rangemaster, and the company, now part of the Aga group, makes little else but modern range cookers and kitchen sinks – in fact the firm is now the largest manufacturer of kitchen sinks in the UK.

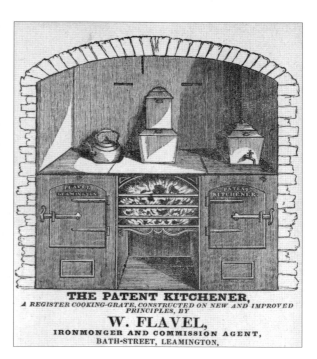

The Elite, with its contemporary appearance and brushed stainless finish, is a popular model among current Rangemaster products. However, historians might find many links between the original kitcheners and the modern Rangemasters, both produced on exactly the same site in South Leamington. Both ranges used the power source in fashion: then coal, now gas and electricity, and a highly skilled, well-directed workforce is just as important today as it was in 1833 when William Flavel set up the Eagle Foundry.

Above: The cemetery in Priory Terrace, Leamington, which is dedicated to the memory of John and William Flavel. When William Flavel died in 1844 he was buried in a tiny cemetery attached to a chapel run by Lady Huntington's Connection (a version of Methodism). The chapel has long since gone but the cemetery remains. William Flavel's grave is near the far wall, on the right, but a yew sapling partly obscures the headstone.

Left: The ladder bridge over the canal near Flavels in 1990. The forerunner of this bridge was built in the 1790s to carry the ancient footpath from Whitnash to Leamington and Lillington. Since Flavels set up the Eagle Foundry in 1833, many workers have used the bridge and footpath to reach work.

six

Proud of our Heritage

Kenilworth sculptor Walter Ritchie with his distinctive work *Flight into Eygpt*. This was installed into the newly completed St Joseph's Roman Catholic Church in Murcott Road, Whitnash, in 1971, and it has been the source of much interest ever since. At one time Walter Ritchie studied under the famous sculptor Eric Gill and he later completed several commissions for the City of Coventry, which was the place of his birth. Examples of his work can also be seen in other parts of England. (Courtesy *Coventry Evening Telegraph*)

Right: Whitnash veterinary surgeon, Alistair Marks, poses with a star patient in 1993. Mac, a two-year-old Staffordshire bull terrier, had been badly injured by a speeding train after he had strayed onto the railway line. It took three operations, around 400 stitches and lots of loving care to bring about his recovery.

Below: Apple Tree Cottage, Doglands Lane, in the 1970s. Looking rather different to the dwellings of sixty years previously, the two thatched houses look extremely attractive and comfortable.

Watts Cottage looked in good repair in the 1960s. However, the property, previously known as Landor's Cottages, was in a terrible state by early 1983. Some beams seemed likely to give way and a massive wooden prop was put in place to prevent any collapse. The property was then owned by St Margaret's Church and the Rector, Canon Anthony Gardner, did all he could to help the situation.

The cottages, fully restored, c. 1992. In 1983 the rundown property was purchased by local builder, Roger Barber, and his wife Lynn. It took three years of restoration work, but by 1987 Cobweb Cottage, as it was renamed, was a very desirable residence.

Roger Barber thatching the roof of Cobweb Cottage in 1985. Having tiled the roof himself, Roger was asked by the planning authority to reinstate thatch as the cottage was a listed building. He sought advice and, rather than incurring expense by employing a master-thatcher, Roger did the work himself, having devised a way of laying thatch over the tiles. (Courtesy *Coventry Evening Telegraph*)

Above: South Farm, not far from the Plough and Harrow, in the 1950s. When the farmland was sold for development, the farmhouse was demolished and a large housing estate was completed over a period of ten years.

Left: The opening of the enlarged Whitnash Medical Centre by Councillor Heath, Mayor of Whitnash, in 2001. Situated in Coppice Road, only a few hundred yards from the site of South Farm House, the premises, first opened in 1984 as a part-time venture, had previously been called South Farm Surgery.

Opposite below: This aerial view, taken in 1994 by Tom Roberts, shows St Margaret's Church at the centre of Whitnash, just as it has been since Saxon times. To the right of the church, surrounded by lawns, stands the modern Rectory, built in 1958, and in the foreground, between the Rectory and St Margaret's House, is the church car park.

The Rector, Canon Anthony Gardner, escorts his daughter Rachel to St Margaret's Church for her marriage to Robert Clifton in 1993. In the background is St Margaret's House, built a few years earlier on the site of a former orchard.

Left: Drummer Alan Wright, of Bishop's Tachbrook, and Whitnash resident Bill Pound, on melodeon, wait for their cue to begin playing. Both were members of Chinewrde, a morris dancing group from Kenilworth. In July 1994 the group performed at a St Margaret's Day celebration in front of St Margaret's Church, the event being organised by the newly formed Whitnash Society in an attempt to revive interest in former customs.

Below: Policewoman Mandy Saysell poses for the local press on one of the Whitnash boundary signs after being appointed to serve Whitnash in 1995. The fact that Whitnash has been twinned with Villebon-sur-Yvette in France and Weilerswist in Germany since 1989 is given great prominence on the signs.

In 1995, a team of morris dancers from Whitnash Combined School gave an enthusiastic display as part of the St Margaret's Day celebrations.

Whitnash Bowlers in 1997. From left to right, back row: A. Segadelli, R. Evans, K. Dolby, G. Barrow, G. Ogilvie, R. Turner, M. Turner, E. Boot, R. Cook, D. Ballard, E. Thompson, ? Raggett, L. Clarkson, G. Cluff, C. Austin, K. Ogilvie, P. Gilbert, D. Thompson, C. Lea, W. Ross, A. Godfrey, W. George, E. Timms, B. Statham, R. Gregory, N. Austin, T. Ankers, E. Perkins, G. Reader, J. Statham, T. Thurlbeck. Front row: J. Ankers, P. Coling, S. Horley, M. Timms, B. Horley, D. Lawrence, S. Raggett, B. Mullally, G. Billington, S. Gilbert, T. Davies, A. Diston, O. Billington. The Mayor was Harry Hughes.

In 1995 Briar Hill Infants' School in Coppice Road celebrated its Silver Jubilee and headmistress Mrs Sarah Lancaster is surrounded by pupils from Class HB7. From left to right, front row: Lucy Frost, Andrew Draper. Second row: Steven Allen, Sunil Kumar, Nicole Miley, Aaron Taylor, Matthew Edward. Third row: Thomas Green, Natalie Watson, Kate Hopkins, Simon Millward, Kate Davis, Andrew Hyde. Back row: Kimberley Cooper, Gavin Taylor, Matthew Taylor, Richard Collis, Stephanie Williams, Jasmin Sandhar, Jennifer Ley.

Above: In 1999, the Whitnash Springers Parent and Toddler Group was visited by the Mayor of Whitnash. From left to right, back row: Kate Pickering with Callum, Mayoress Vera Stocks and Elain Halsey with Gemma. Middle row: Pollyanna, Melissa, James, Olivia and the Mayor, Councillor David Stocks. Front row: William, Daynor, Amy, Charlotte, Hannah.

Left: The 300-year-old Boundary Oak continued to flourish in 1997. In 2000 when a cycle track, footpath and houses were being constructed nearby, an area round the canopy of the impressive tree was fenced in for protection. Later the Whitnash Society organised a display board pointing out the significance of the tree, and the resulting press coverage made it better known.

Right: In 1994, Eric Price of Kenilworth showed his skill by renewing a rush seat on an old chair belonging to a Whitnash resident. The demonstration took place in Whitnash Library as one of a series of events celebrating rural life, organised by Warwickshire County Council. (Courtesy of *Coventry Evening Telegraph*)

Below: Jackie and Stan Warmington celebrated their ten-year involvement with the Whitnash Society in 2004. Jackie was chairman for a time in 1994 and later her husband completed ten years in that position. Formed in 1993 with Ian Box as secretary, the Whitnash Society has since been very active, especially in protecting the historical remains of an old watermill and the rural beauty of the Whitnash Brook Valley.

Above: In 1997 Bernard Kirton became the first councillor from Whitnash to be elected chairman of Warwickshire County Council. The appointment had added significance because an old legend linked the Ragged Staff of Warwickshire with Whitnash. Morvidus, Earl of Warwick many centuries ago, is said to have slain a giant with a young ash tree, which he tore up by its roots. Some historians have suggested that the sapling came from Whitnash, as one meaning of the name of the town is Splendid Ash.

Left: The band of St Margaret's Junior School took part in the St Margaret's Day celebrations in 1998. The trumpeter was Stephen Hands.

Lauren Waterhouse, aged seven, performing an Irish dance in July 1998. Each of the four primary schools in Whitnash agreed to contribute to the St Margaret's Day celebrations and St Joseph's Roman Catholic School volunteered to give a display of dancing on the green.

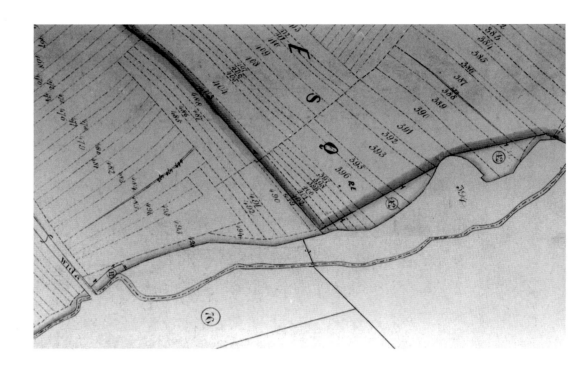

A symbolic photograph taken in April 2003 when the Mill Dam Meadow finally opened as a Nature Reserve, under the stewardship of Warwickshire Wildlife Trust. In the group are Gordon Nichols (with hand raised), current Chairman of A.C. Lloyd, the developers who built many of the houses in Whitnash and Sydenham during the past five decades. Also pictured are Joe Short, Mayor of Whitnash, (right) and Balvinder Gill, Chairman of Warwick District Council (centre). Walking behind, from left to right, are Bernard Kirton, Jackie and Stan Warmington of the Whitnash Society, and Andy Tasker, Chief Executive of Warwickshire Wildlife Trust. In Victorian times, the area alongside the brook was a little-used meadow where Canon Young found and catalogued wildflowers for one of the first books on the flora of Warwickshire. That this area remains relatively unspoilt today is a tribute to all concerned.

Opposite above: A map of the Mill Dam Meadow area from the Inclosure Award map in 1850. The old strip system of agriculture was finally abolished in Whitnash far later than in most other places. Here the brook (with a dotted line down the centre) marks the boundary between Whitnash and Radford Semele. The long thin area of the Mill Dam Meadow was left uncultivated because it was sometimes flooded and was uneven as it contained the site of a medieval dam and watermill.

Opposite below: An aerial view of the same area, taken by Tom Roberts in 1994, at the request of the Whitnash Society. The houses on the top left corner are those of South Sydenham.

Other local titles published by Tempus

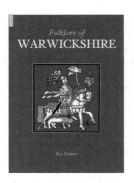

Folklore of Warwickshire

ROY PALMER

Warwickshire is a county steeped in tradition, folklore and mythology. Revised from the original, this new illustrated edition is a fascinating study of folklore rooted firmly within the context of popular culture and history. There are tales of saints and sinners, sports and pastimes, fairs and wakes, folk song and balladry, as well as the passage rites of marriage, birth and death.

0 7524 3359 8

Warwickshire CCC 100 Greats

ROBERT BROOKE

Since Warwickshire's first and only bona fide cricket club was formed at Leamington Spa's Regent Hotel on 8 April 1882, it has enjoyed a chequered record of success and failure. There can, however, be no argument about the individual ability of the players who have represented the club over the decades. This volume looks back and recognises the achievements of the men whose contributions made the county.

0 7524 2180 8

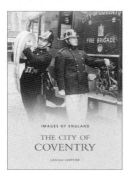

City of Coventry

GRAHAM KEMPSTER

This collection of 170 archive photographs are drawn from the archives of the *Coventry Evening Telegraph*; the local daily newspaper which has served the people of Coventry since 1891. They highlight some of the important events that have occurred in the city during the last century, including blitz bombing during the Second World War, and the arrival of the railway at the end of the nineteenth century.

0 7524 3357 1

Stratford Blue
A history of Stratford-on-Avon's Local Buses

ROBERT L. TELFER

Stratford Blue was founded in 1927 and its buses were a familiar sight in Warwickshire and across the border into Gloucestershire, Oxfordshire and Worcestershire for almost forty-five years. This comprehensive history of the company is sure to appeal to transport enthusiasts and passengers alike.

0 7524 2792 X

If you are interested in purchasing other books published by Tempus, or in case you have difficulty finding any Tempus books in your local bookshop, you can also place orders directly through our website

www.tempus-publishing.com